MW01277989

FRAGRANCE

A Woman's Garden of Verse

Veda Mata M. Ed.

Copyright © 2013 by Veda Mata
First Edition – November 2013

ISBN
978-1-4602-1904-1 (Paperback)
978-1-4602-1905-8 (eBook)

All rights reserved.

Copyright of Veda Mata, 2013
Property of author Veda Mata
Victoria, B.C., Canada

No portion of this book my be printed or used without permission of the author
who can be contacted at vedamata@hotmail.com

No part of this publication may be reproduced in any form, or by any means,
electronic or mechanical, including photocopying, recording, or any information
browsing, storage, or retrieval system, without permission in writing from the
publisher.

Produced by:

FriesenPress
Suite 300 – 852 Fort Street
Victoria, BC, Canada V8W 1H8

www.friesenpress.com

Distributed to the trade by The Ingram Book Company

Table of Contents

to Oriole

The golden hours on angel wings
flew o'er me and my dearie
As dear to me as light and life
is my sweet [Oriole] Mary

Robert Burns

FRAGRANCE

MY GARDEN

A GARDEN is a lovesome thing, God wot!
Rose plot,
Fringed pool,
Ferned grot –
The veriest school
Of peace; and yet the fool
Contends that God is not –
Not God! in gardens! when the eve is cool?
Nay, but I have a sign;
"Tis very sure God walks in mine."

T. E. Brown

BLOSSOM

The tips of Mother's apron strings
Have long been left behind
The warmth I felt within her skirts
Rests still, within my mind
As voices softly calling me
Alone into the night
Remind me she is there no more
To hold me ever tight
Against her breast
Laden with sweet milk

I was a blessed child secure
And loved within parental arms
First daughter
Born of early afternoon
Came out of late spring blossomings
Before the first note of
June sprung clear
In the meadowlark's song

May child
I bore a flower's smile
That carried the day long light
Far into the darkness of the night
Where eyes of loneliness
Were yet to be found
A joy that rests there yet
Accompanying me as a friend
Will rest no doubt 'til journey's end
Where Death as mother
Will gather me into her frocks
Of velvet, dark and real
The journey round the seasons
In and out of circles

Dark and bright
Carrying me down paths
Where I had yet to tread alone
Forsaken often by my friends
Will lead me yet to places
Where I alone must be

In face of visions and of dreams
Which I have long since dreamt
As if a knowledge
Had forewarned my sight
Guiding me into that moment
Where all takes place
As if it were meant to happen
All previously planned

This certainty of future cast
Chambered deep inside
Was born beyond my eyes
Upon the moment that
I thrust forth from Mother's womb
That first breath of recognition
Abiding now
Within subconscious drawers
Latent until the point
Where dream and reality meet
At crossroads
Where I meet my Self

And realize that I
Within the shadows of the night
Was not lost, but wandering
Meandering alone
To greet the brightness
Of the morning's light

A single glance ahead
A reassuring touch
Towards the silver thread
Black fears of loneliness dissolve
Visions of unknown adventure evolve
Onward along the walk towards the garden
And the flowerbed . . .

The crumbs need not be dropped
Upon the forest floor
As birds would only eat them anyways
No more a need to return
To spaces long since past
At long last
The thought of Mother's kiss
Is enough
To procure new strength
In reminiscing
Within my womb
A reborn power arising

A room within myself
Where I alone may feel
The beauty of that childish smile
Upon my lips, real
Sudden wholeness reveals itself
Expression of a happiness
Empty spaces filled with joy
Enveloped in new found womaness

BUFFALO BEANS

Once upon a merry day
A meadowlark jumped out to say
"Come follow me into the heart
Of spring and mother nature!"

I hesitated first and then
My fears flew off with Meadow's tune
I leapt to feel the spring in me
And danced about the room

I was surprised to sense the glee
My spirit flew so joyfully
To long past jaunts and
Places of my childhood haunts

Remembering the robin's song . . .
His red breast bobbing up and down
As he heart-fully hopped along
Encouraging oh so cheerfully

Once more he stepped across my path
Now looked me in the eye
As if to say "I dare you come
Along this bye and bye!"

I thought a moment there
And then I spread my wings
We flew into another world
That past remembering brings

We landed where the buffaloes roam
With crocuses galore

Their purple puffs so soft and bright
Arrayed the grassy floor

I chanced beside the gopher hole
Discovered once when young
When I was but a little girl
Around the age of ten

I knew my mother told me
Not to go away too far
She was afraid I might get lost
By following my star

Dangers lay beyond the home
That's why she said I must not roam
Beyond the gates where
She could keep me sound and safe

The robin glanced at me again
So challenging he looked
I smelled the scent of Buffalo Beans
And knew that I was hooked

The gopher poked his head out side
And sniffed the fragrant air
Then invited me to step inside
To enjoy his favourite chair

The robin nodded "Yes!"
So sure that this was good
I wondered if his winged charm
Was foolish and if I should

But then I braved that certain step
With hope jumped in the hole
Dark and fecund though it was
I trusted my own soul

Faith's guiding hand put me into
A familiar space where I just knew
The gopher's hole was the place to be
And trust the gift she offered me

To tell you true we enjoyed some ham
And biscuits marmalade and jam
A jolly time was had by all
Before I heard the robin's call

Time had come to fore to say
Tea time was ending for today
Dark clouds were forming in the sky
Rain was looming bye and bye

Spring's promise of life journeys
Whet our appetites for more
Continuation and imagining
What the weather had in store

Overhead the gloaming
A rainbow, stretching forth
Across the showering horizon
Pointing back towards the north

I looked again to find
The crocus hats and yellow beans
The robin reached to touch my arm
Time to return it seemed

Where was I at and did I mind?
To leave the meadows far behind
To fly with faith and hope
And see my way back home

For I had found the courage
To travel on the rainbow ring
And listen to spring's melody
Of notes that some larks sing!

ROSE

Rose you are dear to me
The sky becomes your colour
It is very clear to me
There is no other flower
Quite so rare to me
You are my soul
Lace your scent within me
Deer–like eyes reward thee
Rose
You take nothing from me
Your petals delicate my touch
As soft as baby's breath
I feel you
It is a joy to know you
Beauty's face
I see you within
The cloudy pastures
Of my brow
Rose

LADY SLIPPERS

It was a misty morning
In and out of drizzling rain
That we paid our final visit
To the fairies on the hill

We were two travelling ladies
Who had come upon a pond
In the mist of northern journeys
Stopped where spring-like waters

Found their way upon earth's surface
Hot and steaming it was bound
To share its gifts with those who
Needed nourishment and love

Now on this day when night was spent
With friends and fires glow
The burning ambers smouldered
As dawn began to show
Its face upon earth's surface
And lighted pathways to the heaven
Like garden on the hill

The path was wet and hard to find
At times it proved a trial
But fairies waiting patiently
Encouraged our ordeal

For there amidst the waterfalls
And clear like pools refreshed
Dawn's fairies started dancing
And this is how they were dressed
The daisies tall and shining

Showed their faces to the sun
Behind the clouds reflected
The petals of their dresses
White and golden centered fun

Their dance was bright and cheerful
Green velvet mosses let
Their tippy toed caresses slip
So merrily they tread

Above the blue belled sadies
Little tinkles dancing tunes
Showered trickling water falls
In simple harmony

The air came clear just as we stepped
To look into the pool
While minnows swam around their home
For laughter made them feel
The gayness of the ball

The buttercups all yellow
Held the hands of sisters white
Who were a little younger
And smaller, it was a sight
To see the fairies dancing all with glee

Low tippy toe we joined them
Our smiles were filled with grace
As one flower in particular
Stepped out to touch our face
"Come join us," they all whispered
And held out something dear
For they were Lady Slippers
Just made for us to wear

"They grow here in the garden,"
The chorus they all sang
"The orchid of our paradise
For you, now let's begin!"

Round and round the fairies danced
Around us in a circle

Their hands were joined in sisterhood
A most unlikely miracle

Now my friend she looked into my eye
But nothing they would miss
"Just laugh and dance," they said to us
"Just join us in our bliss."

"Our waters and our grasses
Our colours and our fun
Are yours for you to gather
Till this sparkling day is done."

We heard them clear and gaily
Never doubting what they said
Silently we shared their step
Our gifts were theirs to lend

We danced and played the morning spent
Our slippers did the trick
That morning we were fairies
Never knowing people's work

Until the time had come to go
The mist arose to fore
My flute had stopped its melodies
They danced us to the door

The final step of waterfalls
We turned to take a look
The fairies, still, were flowers
And our dancing slippers gone

Away the time was spent
Our thankful wishes past
Our lips in silent memory
We slipped back on our way

That ended our experience
The fairies had released
Their gayness with our spirits
We left the hill in peace

A POSY FOR FRIEND

If whenever we depart
The presence of each other's heart
May the mind's eye still behold
The light of springtime and July

If the petals of the rose
From full blossom lightly fall
May the season soon arriving
Softly tint the changing moon

For my thoughts of you blow gaily
As the summer's gentle breeze
My soul is bound to travel with you
Wherever easefully you go

Lasting pleasures often follow
On the lonely path we tread
On dusty roads there sometimes scatters
Pebbles bright familiar stones

Memory's branches like to waver
Though the blossom withers fast
Yet the smells and sights to savour
Long beyond the mourning light

If perchance you go yet harshly
Departures taken ill at ease
My good blessings travel with you
And your path be shed with love

For I born of springtime showers
Delicate my waters be

Freely flourish rosebuds plenty
While there is the young bud's thirst

You are like the rose bush beauty
Perennial flowering your heart
And I am just small one of many
Partaking in your dream

FANCY THAT!

The butterfly has golden wings
Of dusk and apricot
She moves them gracefully to sounds
Of violets and forget-me-nots

The primrose stands upon her toes
To wave as she goes by
"She is a flighty love," they say
"That golden butterfly!"

Around she flies within the air
The blue skies up above
The leaves they say it won't be long
Before she meets her love

And whispers from the wind heard tell
That he comes from the north
His wings of dawn and crimson red
Sing loud of merit and of worth

That is the song of doves abroad
That share the beauty of the wing
The two will meet upon the dust
Alighted on the rainbow ring

FORGET-ME-NOTS

Forgotten
Are those passing days
When innocence stood free
To look at life in kindliness
And face humanity

Long spent
Are thoughts of openness
As flowers to the sun
Blue ones
That closed their petalled brow
Tonight I close my heart
And pray
That with the coming of the day
I'll walk again in sunbeam's path . . .

I mind that Life has changed her face
To frown upon my smile
Her windward song
Is blowing north
And chills my heart
Cold
Blessed I feel its strength
My test
To follow her?
Or sit beneath the sun raised sky

And worship her?

A DRIED BOUQUET OF BLEEDING HEARTS

Now that I think
Of you as passing

Leaves that rest
Dying
Surround my footsteps

Colouring my season
As aging skin
The toughness
Bearing past life

But you left
Less than that
Behind

No image clear
And thoughts of loving
Do not crackle easily

Nor so vividly

More of a crunch

It's over
Between
Yesterday and tomorrow

Time has split the hearts
As eventually it will
Wither the leaves
To dust

Fertilizing tomorrow
Growth
Into a flourishing tree

Your life inside me now

Tomorrow's child
Will dance
Among fallen branches

SUNFLOWER

You are the sun
Momentarily shining
Into my glory
Kindling my joy

You are the fire
Searing the edges
Of my confusion
Burning through
The surface of my defences

Your might reaches
Far into the twilight
Where my heart
Has taken shelter
Discovering the spark
That ignites my inspiration

From a seedling I have grown
Into an unveiling
Blossom that absorbs
The energy
Your presence provides

As if left in a cooler
To prevent the bud from opening
The warmth of your heart's offering
Has taken me off hold

As I feel each petal
Emerging, taking shape
Spreading out
Into its proper place

I attribute my fullness
To the grace of your light

CHINESE PRINT

The floral rooster descends
Upon the white swans' dive
Its clawed approaches defend
Their feathered glide

As light lily's silent music
Sweet the scent of silent tones
Loud the laughter of the colour
Beaked pursuit of those below

Cantons' dragon China lilies
Moonlike blue and cloudy skies
Earth and heaven's lot rotation
Winged flight blighted eyes

Encantation like ascendance
Peaceful but confused it swells
Universes dance in glory
While the heart of darkness dwells

Confusion has no place here
Where clearness dissolves fear

TRANSLUCENCE

Like a lone magnolia flower on a leafless branch
I teeter on the edge as the winds of life pass me by

I can feel the browning of my edges
Since the height of my glory has slipped down time

Yet the fragrance and beauty of the pink and white blossoms linger
And the delicate traces cling to a light in my memory

Back to time long spent of peace and contentment
Time when youth was blazing with the effervescence of spring

Time before the caverns of the heart filled with sorrow
Where the deep recesses of darkness spilled over in tears

Cleansing and washing the old wounds and present loneliness
Unlocking the nightingale that refused to sing while caged

The magnolia blossom speaks of hardiness and presence
Perched and presenting itself to the sun and the onlooker's glance

Perchance there is recognition of qualitative likeness
A bonding of essentialities a remembering of originality

Pearl of moonbeams and solstice imaginings as weeping gives way
To open space melancholic melody and fragile beauty

From the moment it is wrenched from its perch upon the lucky stance
The petals revolt wither shrivel in their occupation towards the earth

Organic fertilizer for future germination rumination collaboration
My consciousness expands to embrace my next life as this flower

THE RECONCILIATION OF JASMINE

Delicate white petals form a quadripodal base
Tethering its center to spray its scent
In the direction of my nostrils

Once I picked a sprig of the same
Along a mica shone path a rocky way back in time

A Grecian island memory
Lingered in love languor and fantastical lore
Bygone days bright with youthful light and frivolous time
Spent before the dawning of responsibility of procreation and maturity

This tiny branch beside my bed set in porcelain
A modern Siam blue vase white remnants of a daughter's journey
Away from home mother and her own threshold of responsibility
Turn the vase around and the scent bares the same fragrance
The same sense of omnipotence ad invincibility

This little sprig found outside the convenience store
Spotted as a dangling along a branch of flowering bush
Covering a cement brick wall between parking lot and hectic street

This smelly gem precisely caught my glance and tickled my nose's fancy
Full aroma jarred me back carried memory to a spot where reluctance
Had not yet been discovered faith hope in life were ribbons on my bonnet
Where future had not yet become yesterday and moments bore fine lines
Of humour blatant honesty sensuous frivolity and flirtatious adventure
With the Parisian tightrope walker and the Sartrian philosopher practising Zen

The union of two scents exactly the same travelling across borders
Of countries time and memory losses the veils dissolve
The experiences merge in a whiff that transports me ethereally
A rediscovery of treasures through scent dual clues

Into a heart that has been touched with momentary peace
And re-establishment

A release from bondage innocent possibilities to transcend form
And become spirit in a moment instead a composite of personal histories
Each moment lives within us stored in the memorably carved crevices
Of hearts curved in time evolving replacing linear direction where
Life becomes a ready dream and time transposes itself in a simple smell.

POPPY SEEDS

Why should I care that communication crosses the lines of color
Why should I care that bridges be built for visions to cross over
Why should I care that people thrive in a world outside of my house
Or that crosses line a horizon steeped in blood
Why should I care that the children dance in fields of glory
Or that poppies remember the joy of rebirth?

SPRING CLEAN-UP!

When I lived with my mother, I used to colour between the lines and wrap
all my ideas in the cellophane of her fear.
When I lived with my mother, I answered to her name and put
all my dreams in the basket of her past.
When I lived with my mother, I wore glasses tinted the same color as her irises.
When I lived with my mother, she held my hand bound by the limitations
of her regret.

When I left home, the rainbows melted and seeped into the future of my hope.
When I left home, the call of the wild sent shivers through the heart of my
imaginings.
When I left home, my eyelids popped with the brightness of the horizon.
When I left home, her apron strings blew circles in the wind.

Now I am middle age, the hues are fading with the flickering glories.
Now I am middle age, my children carry the memory of my relinquished desires.
Now I am middle age, my short sightedness increases with the debit of my
disappointment.

Now I am middle age, the second wind flutters as yet, with expectant reality.

PSALM FOR LEMON BALM

A sheep is lost
Near the stream of disappointment
Past hunger and thirst
Beside the still waters
Weary she rests
Calming her aching breast
Yea
The river has stopped rushing
Time's being
Draws invisible lines
Separating beginnings and ends
The call beckoning home
The comforting voice
Intonates the lull
Before the breeze of inspiration
Spurts blood
And the rod of willingness
Walks with the staff of hope

DAFFODIL

Trumpeter of the morning
Strumpet of the glorious dawn
Blazing beauty of eagerness and youth
A rising start to the Spring of Life
You blare your colour
With the striking bellow of yellow freshness
The heart of new found long lost joy awakening
Shivering the depths of Winter's
Shroud and eternal burrowing
A way from reaction

"Come ye, come ye, one and all
This here is Springtime's call
Enough of dread and slow decline
Lean on my effervescent time!"

"Tune up and awaken cheer
To the heart of the matter, dear."

Life springs and rises to the call
A melody. . . encouraging . . . a turning
Towards the gayness of the light

Fly the green and sunshine banner
Join the herald of the uprising
One more time!

LILY

The lily is aroused from sleep
And wants to open
Her petals to the sun

She hears the beat and blossoms
Her petals to the dance
She shivers to the claps of Thunder

Her lightness reverberates the Calling
Her tears release the power of the morning pain
Lightly on her feet she treads
Around the threatening
Storm

And settles contentedly into
The safety of the circling Drum
Humming the beat
Embracing the rhythm
Of the humming bird's wings
And the skylark's song
Yearning and singing
For Peace

RAPSODY OF THE MORNING GLORY

The sun is rising
Stand to face the East
Raise your hands with Glory
And march towards the dawn

Side by side
Hands flung towards the sky
We turn to face each other
Clasping our fingers in unison
We dance in the morning rays

What is this new togetherness?
What is this familiar otherness?
Where do the boundaries lie
Between yesterday and today?
Between today and tomorrow?
Is there an in-between for us?

Silhouetted against the matin story
The sun is surely rising on a new day
How to define what lies between us?
All that binds us
Gilding our common ground
Spaces where hearts meet
Face to Face
Deep into the other's eyes we search
For depths unknown and unfettered
Gleaning meanings and soul retrievals

Cherishing time
To taste the splendour of new found love
And long lost hopefulness
How do we begin to walk towards the East

Leaving the past to meander towards
The sunset of yesterday's alliances
And unforgotten memories?

What are our possibilities?
Can broken hearts mend
Together a new life?
Only time will tell the answers
Created by our willingness
To embrace love's grace
And turn towards the resplendent dawn

SPRING TALE OF A SNOWDROPS MAKING

I picked two snowdrops
That looked like viper's wands
Or pea-shelled trinkets of content
And placed them on a winter's day
That filled the pages of dismay
With Present's tune, which meant
None other than surprise
That spring was casting shadows
Sprung from earthly bulbing motion
I had the notion that I was here
To spot the tale and sprout its colour
Before the word got out
That there were other flowers
Coming

They told me of the greenish whisper
That matched the fuchsia dwelling
Of petalled future's summoning
Upon the tips of wings and winds
Their words were uttered silently

I heard the voices in the air
But wondered if the birds were only fooling me
Until the whitened arm reached out
To touch the smile of my bewilderment

Could it be that life was really here to share?
My disbelief was so surprisingly bare
I heard the laughter of the floral delicates
As if mocking my disarray of feathers
"Friends," I heard them say
"We are friends of yours to stay!"

IRIS

Daughter of morning
Glory
Spring within
The fountain
Of youth and adventure
Sun amidst the heart
Of Song
Melodies leaping
From centers vast
Soft as the petals
That lick the tiger's tongue
Provocative as the lips
That caress desire's longing
An essence
Of opening
Escapades
Upon delight's fantasy
Intriguing luring enveloping
The phallus of wisdom
The heart that streaks the horn's
Masquerade

Her voice resonates
Memories of time
Forsaken
Forms of dormant visions
Spiralling lines
Where souls have met
In the unity of dance

Dance thou Iris
Of nocturnal censure
Dance thou flower
Of fertility

Womb of delight
Daughter of the rainbow
Absorb my wonder
Play upon my strings
While I abandon
My will
At your leisure

MERRY GOLD

"I am enchanted
oh glorious day
to think that you have taken the time
to shine my way

Oh Oh glorious sun
shine your face upon my land
for I am standing open face
to watch your move

Your yellow sunbeams
glint my eyes with lightness bright
wouldn't you know you chose my face
to shine on

Skipping under your beauty rays
I am delighted to feel you
light-hearted you make me feel
the real you

Oh sunny sunshine play
play my song and feel my heart
beating time
within your tone

Not even the moon can make me feel
so good
you are today's special
happy friend I feel your warmth

So here's my hand let's dance
together you and I

just lead me on rayonly
and I will follow your path!"

"SHAMELESSNESS! REDRESS!"

Casting off the last vestiges of Propriety
The Earth Goddess unmasks the veils
Illusion drops to reveal a full-blooded
Full-throated Feminine Kourosian form
That strikes the edge of boldness as fervour and eroticism
Advance the consciousness across the lightening threshold
Of the new Millennium and back into the depths of darkness
Where the conglomerate of ages defy time.
Space steps forward to exonerate her Liberty
Power of the Shadow! Her emergence into visibility is
Slippery, the fluidity and invincibility of Creative form.

She stands bold upon the horizon of intention
Warrior Woman beyond measure, an intuitive breast
Of unending resources; her intelligence bears secrets
To unravel and diffuse the ignition of Reality's impending holocaust.

Strike the harp! Clash the cymbals!
Set a march in motion!
Thrust the notion of madness into the burning pyre!
Hurtle out invitations; embrace her heart; offer your arms!
Before she takes off, in heat, to the forest.

JOURNEY ALONG THE EDGE OF THE RAINBOW

RED
She has cut the diamond of hope along the windows
Of dreams, angled it into a jewel of vision
Polishing it to reflect and filter projections and expectations
They say she lives in a glass house, a fantasy world, an ostrich
With her head in the sand the real world passes by
Really resilience to buffer the suffering of lost souls
That's youth

ORANGE
Balls of fire hurtled across the horizon of innocence
Searing heart – breaks
How many now have left her behind
Searching for something less than accountable
She now carries a staff and is marching to the pipes of desire and peace

YELLOW
Bellied lizards scattering quickly beneath her feet
She strides the earth challenging the norm
The princess no longer calls her suitors to the castle
There is no longer a price to offer
It has been extracted from the placenta of her womb
She waves her wand and light streams across the horizon of her hope
Fellow man has not lost his attraction
Only now her vision sees beyond the limitations
Relationships' glories can no longer hold her interest

GREEN
Naturally the earth has bled to solar rhythms
Babies in arms the going is harder
Footsteps left dying in the dust

Droughts and crack and rain muddies water
Dried rivulets in time dance around the crow's feet of her eyes
That still squint towards the sun expecting spring
Time passes only hints but the way is paved with bold intentions
Peace and mercy are the refreshments served at this one's party

BLUE
Blue is the color of her true love's hair
Imaging the depth of the seas and the strength of the waves
Her heart is on Krishna and love beyond measure
Not the relatives at home in their material madness
Oil and ooze and trailers at the lake
Multiple cars and mortgages
There is more to life than corporate adventure
Desire's hold is slipping as her grasp on consciousness strengthens
The test is in the teaching
The teacher is now dressed to the nines; she is ready

INDIGO
Three eyes instead of two make the going seem easier
She has met some other adventurers along the way
Tails to trunks to tails and on the elephant parade marches past
Their souls have met and are gone the caravan to glory shines
Out beyond night's end they march and sway
Praying they'll meet others along the way
Humanity together shines over the confusion of the times
Tests are theirs but met together cannot but refute the oncoming storm
Striding against the norm a will that shreds the context of the night
Her will undaunted flaunts itself against the masses' infringing cowardice

VIOLET
Alone again she has advanced beyond the boundaries of others
Clouds stream across the midnight colour of the sky
The moon full awaits untold glory glistening filigree upon the rippling waves
The ocean is potent with secrets and promises
Tomorrow is another day and the future will unfold as it may
There is no knowing only being within momentous form
Strategy and planning will not aid in the awakening
Patience, endurance, and faith that life's tests will present themselves
As surely as the sun will rise with the coming dawn

Hope is tied to the end of the rainbow that brings it full circle
Round and round the millennium of time weaving its ribbons of light
Refracting itself in and out of innocent vision that chooses to follow the Dream

REQUIEM OF LAVENDER

Fields forever stretching across the landscapes of inner vision
Middle age has humped along towards the purple meadows
And sits aging amidst the embracing fragrance of solace and comfort
There is no other place to be at this slip in time

Looking back in hindsight nothing could have been changed
Forces unseen moulded and sculpted the structures
Of incarnation into a bouquet of memorable lessons
Tying ribbons around the bundle as a symbolic victory
Although other's eyes may have interpreted the efforts differently

Rest awhile longer inhaling the lovely scent of contentment
Meanderings down memory's lanes no longer draw
The soul, weary of concentrated efforts to improve and reshape
Longingly caresses the tips of Lavender
Unlocking its gifts unleashing perfumed sighs of peace
Tantalizing the nostrils encouraging soporific bliss and dreaminess

Is this the way to encourage the story
And motivate the will towards completion?
The soft touch of Lavender invades the imagination
Sensing reluctance to sacrifice the moment into action
The rest a question mark a bemused smile and gratitude

Lavender is a tickler tempting the sneeze if taken in large doses
At best a remedial prescription for relaxation and antidote to depression
A potent herb for healing cuts and wounds

And children think it is a flower for Grandmas

SCARLET LETTERS

Dusk and Dawn are lovers
who meet at midnight
on the edge of secrecy
they rendezvous on the tip of darkness
set between the waxing and the waning
where there is no moon to enlighten
the curious onlookers and disbelievers
no moon to shed light
upon their intriguing imagination
of occasions and fascinations

Love
making and refreshing the day each day
splendour
under the vacant moon
rewarding resplendent glory
why not I ask?
they frolic to the tune of the nightingale
which I must admit
I have never actually seen or heard
but have read and reread
alluded to in poetry
this eternal fidelity outlasts
poetry written to capture it
futile exercises in aggrandisement
this love far outreaches a poet's efforts
towards immortality
stretches towards the end of time
with certainty that nature and universal truth
will prevail

Under the cloak of immense darkness
that spreads itself flat out across the skies
hiding from the sparkling stars of the milky way

they plot the landscape's awakening
the splash of beauty's reawakening enchantment
the collusion of patron saints
the Sun awaits the verdict of their intercourse
the fruit of their womb
the re-emergence of radiance

Aurora's blessings showered
upon the nightscape of the wickedness
deceit and disheartenment
that lurks within the potent heart
of darkness
once again exposed
by the magic of morning glory
heralding victory banners
ribbons and rays
flaunted across the skies
by a startling hussy
accompanied by her evening lover
the tempter, the light snatcher
embraced by his faith in her story

Exhaltantly they march across the horizon
their imagining returning excitedly
expectantly towards future
midnight madness and the coming
of the sheltering moon
their post-coital severing
inclining towards the hidden
faculties latent within the darkest moment
ever present blackness
their utmost yearning, entrancing, alluring
awards reunion
blasts false promises
of strength in darkened illusions
fracturing the power tricking the fallacy
of night's perpetual significance

Nothing to compare
love springs eternal
as ever faithful day light
returns to instigate itself
as long as love remains
the heart of darkness

will continue to refute victory
and light's fanciful omnipotence
will continue

All because two lovers remain faithful
to eternity and clandestine adventures.

I WISH I MAY I WISH I MIGHT

I blow a dandelion to the wind
And wish with all my might
That you were here beside me
To share this lovely night

I listen to the music
Which opens up my heart
And feel the space's vacancy
For you to take your part

I weep at separations
And wonder why they are
It hurts to see the darkness
Behind the falling star

I want for us to shine so bright
Beside each other true
To feel our freedom's fancy
Hand in hand, just me and You

The seeds all scatter to the wind
To plant Love lost from sight
And no foretelling says I can't
Just have the wish I wish tonight!

SNOW FLOWERS

It seems to me
That even though
The winter's come at last
I dream of springtime blossomings
And seasons long since past

I see before my weary eyes
The ocean's view and cloudy skies
The calm before the thunderstorm, still
Threatening the golden petalled daffodil

Innocent life continues on
Is sung within summer's song
The bluebird's tune has flown away
To come again another day

When leaves begin to sprout anew
And sunrise glistens through the dew
Creating rainbow patterns upon the blades
And grass begins to grow again

But now the autumn's gone for sure
The leaves once red and golden brown
Are now seen lying low upon the ground
Mixed with sidewalk grey and brittle trees
There is no doubt within my mind
That winter's really here

Bells of Christmas sound the air
As coloured lights more colourful
Award the coming end of year
A celebration, forgotten cheer

And lastly look to snowflakes falling
Faintly sounding reason
To note the changing of the season
White silver petals
Laden life upon the windows
Crystal flowers of winter's calling

Gladly voicing her beauteous treasures
Silently within the crisp night air
The spirit of Noel has come
To share with all who hear
Her quiet music - promising gladness
Of the coming year

A LAUREL GARLAND
OF THANK YOUS

About the Book

Fragrance, a collection of poems written over the course of Veda Mata's adult life, is a culmination of a heart's dream. It is a floral display of a life well spent and the seasons of a faithful heart. Each poem radiates like a jewel with the essence of Veda's spirit and vision of her life. This compact book is an honest cultivation of the garden of life through poetic expression, exemplifying the spirit of renewal and transformation. It is a tribute to the strength and beauty of the feminine and to the resurgence of spring. As a depiction of the eternal flowering of the human spirit, it exudes a delightful fragrance of faith, hope, and clarity.

About the Author

Veda Mata, M. Ed. is a Reiki Master, Meditation Instructor, and Spiritual Life Coach. She lives in Victoria, B.C., Canada where she completed her B.A. in English Literature and Master Degree in Education, specializing in Tibetan Buddhism and the Teaching of Compassion as exemplified by the Dalai Lama. She devised a Pedagogy of Happiness based on Buddhist ideas of Consciousness development.

Veda chooses to live in Victoria, near her children and grandchildren who are a constant source of joy and happiness. She enjoys meandering the flower lined streets of this lovely city, aptly named the Garden Capital of Canada. It is not surprising that Veda has chosen flowers as her favourite analogy. To her, they represent the essence of beauty on earth and are a true reflection of the preciousness of life.

Fragrance is Veda's second book. Her first, *Knocking On Buddha's Door*, is a novel memoir about her spiritual adventures into the heart of India and Nepal. Both books can be ordered through vedamata@hotmail.com.

CPSIA information can be obtained
at www.ICGtesting.com
Printed in the USA
LVOW12s2250160916

505008LV00001B/5/P